Dear Z:

THE ZYGOTE EPISTLES

Also by Diane Raptosh

Human Directional (Etruscan Press, 2016)
American Amnesiac (Etruscan Press, 2013)
Parents from a Different Alphabet (Guernica, 2008)
Labor Songs (Guernica, 1999)
Just West of Now (Guernica, 1992)

Raptosh's America is razor-wired by Netflix subscriptions, mass shootings, "mouthy and awful" loving, and the digital grift of a click economy masquerading as a heart but shaped like a blob and hell-bent on commercializing everything in its path. In *Dear Z: The Zygote Epistles*, we inherit a crushing reckoning with the human experiment, "the self on the one hand, / a cell phone, the other," as we direct our bodies, sometimes feebly, sometimes with a swiped-in grace, "toward the arms / of the moans . . ." This is a collection simultaneously anchored to the past and miraculously stretching forward, along the Ethernet cables, into what is entirely, brazenly, Raptosh's time.

—J. Reuben Appelman, *Make Loneliness* and *The Kill Jar*

Dear Z is a book of dynamite. Or rather, "a hot load of humanity ammo." What kind of world will a forming zygote be born into? Should we form a zygote to bring into this kind of world? Raptosh's epistolary apostrophes address the "life speck" nestled in her niece's womb as a "spec life," and their speaker, who nestles in the "mind's womb" of embodiment, is decidedly of two minds about that: "Flesh is the not-me / I peacock around in." She is tender: "the *me* there is *you* sized." She is juicy and passionate: "it's me . . . you know: the one with the raw wrath-wantonness issues." But above all she is dazzlingly, breathtakingly acute: pure high-energy verbal swerve. Invoking the moral scaffolding of *Moby-Dick* and lexes from symbolic logic to hip-hop, no line in the book fails to proliferate on second reading. Raptosh proves a masterful mistress of the subtle pun and proverb; the velocity of her sleights of word will leave the reader replete . . . But it also suggests that a world that can embody a mind like this just might be worth being born into.

—Randall Couch, *Peal*

It takes courage to start a book of poems with an explanation of *Moby-Dick*. But it takes something else, some kind of serious playfulness, to address that book to the "Dear Zygote," even as it transforms into "Life Speck," with side moments as "Zeitgeist," "Zero," or even "teensy homunculus." Yes, there's humor in all of this wordplay, but I prefer the older term, "wit"—with its implications of gentleness, even of wisdom. In all the wordplay and wisdom of *Dear Z*, we are reminded in every poem that it is addressed to that "life speck," to the possibility of the future, to its own kind of hope.

—Keith Taylor, *The Bird-while*

Zygote, zeitgeist: "What we call world is also—perhaps more accurately—called the *without*." *Dear Z* barebacks the language that made us human, showing how it is making us super- (as in, in-) human—or at the very least, why a terrestrial translator is needed to usher a "Life Speck," a "spec consciousness," into modern humanity, which begins with *Moby-Dick*, or, "likely East Africa 200,000 / years ago" and hurtles through our rampage to "the Zombies, who borrowed / from Big Mama Thornton and copied Sam Cooke," landing on *"Ameri-pire's endpoint,"* where *"person* / comes uncoupled / from the rank of *citizen."* As Raptosh cautions, "Hang on to the winch of all this shape-shifting!"

—Megan Levad, *What Have I to Say to You*

Dear Z:
THE ZYGOTE EPISTLES

Diane Raptosh

etruscan press

Etruscan Press
Wilkes University
84 West South Street
Wilkes-Barre, PA 18766
(570) 408-4546

 Wilkes
University

www.etruscanpress.org

Published 2020 by Etruscan Press
Printed in the United States of America
Cover image: *Math Mapping* © Nadine 'Yadi' Royster
Cover design by Lisa Reynolds
Interior design and typesetting by Julianne Popovec
The text of this book is set in Palatino Linotype.

First Edition

17 18 19 20 5 4 3 2 1

Library of Congress Cataloguing-in-Publication Data

Names: Raptosh, Diane, author.
Title: Dear Z: the zygote epistles / Diane Raptosh.
Description: Wilkes-Barre, PA: Etruscan Press, 2020.
Identifiers: LCCN 2018020970 | ISBN 9780999753453
Classification: LCC PS3568.A634 A6 2020 | DDC 811/.54--dc23
LC record available at https://lccn.loc.gov/2018020970

Please turn to the back of this book for a list of the sustaining funders of
Etruscan Press.

This book is printed on recycled, acid-free paper.

*This book is dedicated to Camas Lee Schaeffer
and in memoriam: Peter Jackson, 1963-2018*

DEAR Z: THE ZYGOTE EPISTLES

Acknowledgments

Grateful acknowledgment to the editors of the journals and anthologies for publishing poems from this collection, sometimes in slightly different form:

Africanization and Americanization: Searching for Inter-racial, Interstitial, Inter-sectional, and Interstates Meeting Spaces, Africa Vs. North America, Volume 1

After Moby-Dick: An Anthology of New Poetry

Bellevue Literary Review

Dark Matter: Women Witnessing

For the Love of Orcas: an anthology

Leviathan: A Journal of Melville Studies

Mantis: A Journal of Poetry, Criticism & Translation

Limberlost Review

Michigan Quarterly Review

with profound gratitude for kindness and support from

J. Reuben Appelman, Philip Brady, Rob Carney, Keats Raptosh Conley, Randall Couch, Diane Jarvenpa, Karen Krumpak, Melissa Kwasny, Megan Levad, Robin Lorentzen, Alan Minskoff, Letty Nutt, John Ottenhoff, Colette Raptosh, Eric Raptosh, Camas Schaeffer, Bill Schneider, Marc Sheehan, Keith Taylor, Pamela Turchin, and Lucinda Wong.

and with gratitude for grants from

the Alexa Rose Foundation and the Idaho Commission on the Arts for travel to the Nantucket Historical Research Library and the Nantucket Whaling Museum in support of research for this book.

Dear Z:

THE ZYGOTE EPISTLES

I

Maybe Moby

Dear Z,

Shit happens   as   Whiteness
     shuffles around

       on its   peg leg.

       whump

This means I will have to teach you
key habits of Melville's whole novel

by borrowing
algebra's alphabet.
Through using some logic equations:

A. Forms of Propositions.

a.   Moby Dick is a whale.
b.   A whale is a mammal.
c.   Moby Dick is Ahab's enemy.
d.   Moby Dick is not the devil.

e.   Ishmael is not albino.
f.   Ishmael is Moby Dick's friend.
g.   Ishmael is not God.
h.   Moby Dick is not a fish.

i.   Moby Dick defeats Ahab.
j.   Ahab is meaner than the devil.
k.   Ishmael is everyone's friend.
l.   Ahab is not Ishmael's enemy.

m.   Moby Dick is albino.
n.   No one is meaner than Ahab.
o.   Ahab is meaner than anyone.
p.   God is not a whale.

q. The devil is no one's friend.
r. Ahab has no friends.
s. Ishmael does not defeat Ahab.
t. God is not the devil.

B. Exceptive Propositions and Superlatives.

a. Everyone except Ahab fears Moby Dick. *(Zxy ≡ x fears y)*
b. No one except Ahab can defeat Moby Dick.
c. Moby Dick is the only albino whale.

d. Only Ishmael is a friend of Moby Dick.
e. No one is meaner than Ahab except the devil.
f. There are no other whales besides Moby Dick that are feared by Ishmael.

Legend ≡ : "is identical to"; ≥ : greater than or equal to; ≅ : congruent to; | | (in later poems) means these two words need to just sit side by side.

Helpful abbreviations.

a = Ahab; d = the devil; g = God; I = Ishmael; m = Moby Dick; Ax ≡ x is albino; Fx ≡ x is a fish; Mx ≡ x is a mammal; Px ≡ x is a person; Wx ≡ x is a whale; Dxy ≡ x defeats y; Exy ≡ x is an enemy of y; Fxy ≡ x is a friend of y; Mxy ≡ x is meaner than y; Sxy ≡ x is swifter than y.

So then. *I = Ishmael.* Oh might as well,
since *x is a mammal,*
and they're pretty quick. Besides which,

as soon as I slip
into cypher's forecastle
I'm free. You cannot undo

the *done-unto-you,*
but you can forgive it. Tonight I'm feeling like
forming ex-expletives,

something like *apeshit's*
shapeshift to lippy-glug happiness.
Zygote, you'll get it:

every egg has an X,
every leg wants a dress,
Moby Dick is no devil,

which means every Ahab
must locate the beings
on whom he can offload the whale

of his own inner torment:
Could be the grave
disease of our day. ... *I = Ishmael.*

Px ≡ x is a person.
A person:
Life Speck, by now,

maybe you're newly sized
to a raw sesame seed.
Already you are

what the world will call *girl*
or a *guy,* but here's the P.S.:
Female = the default sex,

probably precisely
because *x is swifter than y,*
where here we let *swift* mean *gifted*

in souped-up stillness. Why is it
Zxy ≡ x fears y? Sometimes *y* really
starts to stick it to *x* and somehow

that's supposed to be *Sxy*. Maybe *y* will get
a chance to leaven himself. ... Sometimes
Moby is only a vegan musician, whereas,

Zygote, I think you more or less
a fish-person, or *FxPx*. Hang on
to the winch of all this shape-shifting!

Being able to sidle the glide of another
is what preserves us. And who would deny
that Biblical Ishmael doubled

as more or less donkey-mankind,
or that Melville's
narrator-self

is spec consciousness?
Sentences are
sentience's avatars,

but alas this plows us into new ships
far at sea. *d = the devil.*
And cruelty's *Mxy*. Both

of them gather as I not-quite
whistle *Ishmael*-Dixie and maybe
twelve nieces shall I beget

who will multiply
all that sits opposite meanness exceedingly,
at the same time as they become

badass in archery. God-*ishness*
is not a whale, isn't something
given to *is*-ing or not, so let us declare-ask

a quotient: *The first*
1,000-year-old person's
already been born?

Zygote, Life Speck,
oh, just say
Everyone: Let's get un-*Exy*.

We're wearing identical tentacles,
and I know I am mapping out days
of my nights through the specs

of my ending-most seconds,
even though I'm not there yet.
This is the way

to place-date me in space-time, there
with the barely conceived —
that fertilized nation

through whose fallopian truths
all manner of things
gain fragility's strength.

There's nothing
that couldn't *not happen*,
world without end

rigging its fishy iFriends,
its runaway jibs,
and yes — sometimes loving

is mouthy and awful
but there's no other force
earnest enough in a world this peckish,

in which x might end up fishibian,
in which x is a mammal
in which x is a kiss

whose finitude gushes
exchange of 80-plus million ginned-up bacteria,
known for their binary fission, their runaway swiftness.

Life Speck,

   Let us let *X* = *mammalian I,*
and to boot an old friend,

which is what chinks us
   to Queequeg, whom Ishmael half
morphs his way into simply

by thinking about glyphs
   harpooned on Q's skin. That Möbius strip
of a person! That cannibal prince

and his code—the ship's crux.
   His wooden doll treatise makes kindness
suggest *Let's go make rainbow fish*

from these minnows!
   Maybe we always only just needed
more liminal structures

from which to untangle mind's lures:
   to re-feel how Queequeg calls us to
cradle new berths for pain

in ways that might lurch us more
   toward the good. In short, Q wants us
to serve as real-time person-assisters—

in 21st-century marketplace parlance—
   whose purlieu could clearly be said
to suffer the Ahab Complex.

Queequeg's epiderm-text
   basically pray-asks whoever picks up a pen
to rewrite the word. Repeat a theme

of joyride beauty. Who wouldn't prefer to
            queue up one's crypto-adventure
across the blaze of each limb,

if only to showcase
            such blue, raw, gnosis-explosion?
It's a little bit *krill swarm*. It's a couple parts tetrapod.

Dear Z,

you're just an old flit

off the infinite-quickie.

You're this age's latest, for realz —

where *latest* means *newness's*

baby. You're it and

you're ≥ it,

X and *not X,*

and that's the *now's* poetry's

loving-most hummingbird

so *ew,* wipe that snore

off your nose in order

to face
the Blue Ocean Event.

Pretend that
you know the drill

of the shell corporations,

those *not-anywheres,* those surpluser nations'

distant money troves. Ho! The shit things

we think to twiddle

our thumb-quickness on:

Reality jousts its own touchscreen,

or maybe it's just some multi-*Sxy* transjester,

and I am // over-above all

offender and victim: In terms of cell transfer,

I am both my son and daughter,

I'm a little Tahlequah, that Orca whale mother,

and my own mom,

plus I'm your great aunt

and therefore your slightly more devilish Ishmael—

$I \cong d,$

this turnstile

sound fiend/word nun-*cum*-rapper.

Oh, self is striptease art,

but the sphere around it is a hearth.

I feel, therefore I think
I am free.

Life Speck—

there is nothing

that can't be done with English

that will not almost quench your anguish.

Dear Z,

MyRapName.com redubs "Zygote" like this:

Z.A. Butter Nugget, AKA *Rich Jam.* And I'll just mention

how much I treasure your grapheme color *here*

at the same time as I name-mourn

the *Saying of Mean Things Practically Everywhere*

our national sickness *du jour*. No doubt you've heard:

There is this crowd-sourced

text, *Emoji Dick,*

and the *X-Men: Apocalypse*

is staging this takeover of tons of kids'

Snapchat lens sets. Why, Melville's own Pip,

who swept the ship clean,

had to go mad—each eon keen-anxious

to crank out its rudeness beatitudes.

Truth forms us

in myriad stitch lengths—

the self: This slow fleet of feeling-tone,

this seafare of subtlest bodies.

P.S. Dark letter Z,

        White-*ish* men

    might want to repeal you

      or cage you

should you be approved

    to move beyond embryo's

coffin life-buoy

     and—averting self-deportation—

      come to full being.

Dear Z,
If you could read, you'd find
among the endless flows

of fragmented info plenty of post-truth's
haste speech—naked as knees.
Before you come to be,

try and rethink the yoke-stroke
state of the cultural genome.
Sometimes only a gloom

heats up the luxury spec house
we hoard from within. Listen.
We're probably a little too *in there* for most,

and as we speak, *outercourse*
registered into the draft
of new words, while *pogo*

serves as teens' tag word
for *one thing you do*
that makes people

want to just ditch you.
Even so, neither/or niece,
Internity might be a region

worth birthing. It's true.
Who never enters his solitude
hasn't a *him* to hone,

no hem to queeg onto.
Would you blanket it
crime along the y chromosome

that so many must move—throat first—straight to that
X-man/Ahab anger, letting all hell
scrunch the noose

around sadness's pray-tell?
I hardly can write when I think
of what happened that June

in Orlando's Pulse Nightclub,
but it's worse to refuse to. Maybe
the warfare suits promised

never to knock up itch-thirsts
for plain acts of grainline reflection. … Slogan-tee that
onto somebody's *What's So* tombstone—your mama's

champion genes busy meanwhile
building up gaudy bod plans
for the human to be—

                                 that probity. That not-yet-eyeful.

Dear Z,

I'd rather kick it right here in
the lee of mind's womb

than do almost anything,
especially in the reverse

snow days of early/mid-
July, when the ancient

snakeskin of impossible
heat makes you stay good

and sunk inside a room
to fix on frustrations linked

to, say, Antarctic watermelon snow.
Warming polar zones mean

good news for a fleck
of red alga, but that's about it.

Put another way, I'm not in
a hurry to go and get busy.

To boot, I'd like to escape
the meme-industrial complex

at the same time
as Raposo Fitness

sends repeat e-messages:
belly-flattening overnight

breakthroughs. … Some days
I just want to sit and wait

for something like language's
medic lay clergy to arrive

with their word ambulances,
red/blue lights awhirl~~

with a pair of patrol cars aiming to
bring to full halt the wholesale

plummet of moral thresholds.
But wouldn't I love to dub

giving too much the gateway drug
through which I could have laid

to grace with millions of gifts
most people living. …

Ah, maybe tonight
I will find a new way

to remind myselves we often
get what we don't want.

Which helps us improve.
This doesn't mean the wind

isn't a little skeptical
about state inclusion.

This doesn't mean America
hasn't become a brand

of chump beer. This doesn't
mean there isn't a blackbird

somewhere near here
in a field of blue camas—

head tipped to the right,
yellow-rimmed eye

trained on the sun—
calling out

every riven thing
about the world

in a grand *Tut Tut*
                                                Tut Tut

                                                                                      Tut

II

Warm Oval Office

Zygote, you are my favorite not-quite person
to talk to, though at times I'd rather swoon

> through quill mums, rangy smoke alarms, or quiet's
> naked palms. Is language anguish-gauge or laughing gas?

>> Correct answer: *yes.* I'm not gonna shit you. The queerness
>> of personhood's something to not quite get used to—pits

> to mark ears; eyes, dark blots. Heart's intellect. Perhaps like you,
> I tell myself that everything about the world is *movie,*

and everything that moves within is *world.* Still, to honor
your sand-silt kinship, I'm starting to pat the earth down

> with both forearms just for some new perspective. Dust nit.
> Poppy seed. Iris mite. Jot off life's manicure stick:

>> You are one glad-ass act of insurrection. Of joy's terrorism.
>> The lilac vestige of linking's musicianship.

Dear Z,

Sometimes you want to just take the tone of the world

    down, scrape the pomp off the circumstance, stop

      the marketplace-micrometeorites' fall

across all the black-and-blue trees. Life Speck, that's why

    I live here, in mind's lining. The *me* there is you-sized. The *you* there,

      wearing my niece's body, is spec life—a good enough state

of anxiety to throw down a party. Today is the Feast Day

    of Marie-Marguerite de Youville, patron of the poor. Mother

      of the underseen. First-ever Canadian declared to be a saint.

We're closest to those we're trained not to see:

    the working dimeless. Denizens of charnel ground. Marine algae.

      The filmy stout infant fish. Dust nests smaller even than this: .

    I spy your one little eye almost leaving. … I see things

because I'm unpaid to. Because I'm a teacher at Who University.

Spec kid, not yet a blastocyst: Okay, I'm not gonna fib.

Life is going to try and turn you

into its bitch, never mind biological sex.

And while we're at it, every mother always

already serves as head of a nation: Within

weeks of conception, cells from both mom

and the fetus dart back and forth~~micro-chimeric.

As for this particular planet:

It's one round-backed guitar you frisk

to tension-test for metaphor. That's it.

Power enacts us into being. To persist

in our persons means we give way to terms

which aim to uproot our own. …

This gets me feeling spasmodic:

makes me want to peck at five species.

                      Each day's a flown bunting. A knife-line.

A breakage: the self on the one hand,
                    a cell phone, the other.

Life Speck, you there?

    Still in that warm oval office,
            like Elvis with Nixon? Listen.

Some days, mind's endometrium
        tries to evict me,
            beguile my person

more toward the mobile production
        of selves, make me
            more saleable: turn

each tine of queued word
        into data. Oho—now my phone
            pules and pulls rank

like a helmeted baby.
        Should I try to ignore
            how it lugs the jowl down,

rips out swaths of plumed heat
        from the creed of companionship?
            It makes me weep in the knees

just to be. *U better believe this,*
        Zyggity Stardust,
            Breath's Neck-stroke,

Egg-Cream Homito. Last question:
        How best might anyone
            scroll down the straightedge

of love's paper light—
        its welcoming, holy
            excruciations?

Dear Z,

What kind of being might you be larger than? So glad you asked:

        those dried brine shrimp—that group of crustaceans,

which go into sleep-states just to be sold

        in hatch-kits as fishbowl pets. AKA: sea monkeys.

Supposed to be able to fight, play baseball, and rise

        from the dead, though you can hardly glimpse them—

even with X-ray specs. Zygote, in our age thinking is seen

        as a lump of cold lotion, mostly a thing

too mutant-dreamy to do. Do you bereave me? Would you

        agree to the use of cookies? Don't you just hate

when the no-good knuckles over the truth? Give me

        your nevermore hand: Let us become oblong

sans-nation transitionals, like those lobe-finned fishibians

in the Canadian Arctic, which evolved to all fours

in waters near the Nansen Sound—upon which hoof-smack's music

moves us nonstop: the Peary caribou. The jutty muskox.

Dear Zygote,

What we call *world* is also—perhaps more accurately—called the *without*.

Life Speck,

Lonesomeness likes to level things

with its known equal sign. Even so,

I swear on your living solitude

I have been busy—

voiding counterfeit fear

as normalized currency.

Am trying right now

to figure   how   to fit all these chits

in one urn at time's end. Tat that

onto your slogan-tees, *Señor* Corporation. …

As for you, Zygote, begin

to gate your onesie community

against Algorithm-God;

worship blues' rhythm-glow only.

Mostly Al Green.

Mind if I fry

some sugar-anger into my tea,

my sweet little bitty?

It's me, your great aunt: You know,

the one with the raw, wrath-wantonness

issues, that rad hat of dread—

33

plus I pack the heat

of three different cell populations

around in my body. That's three generations.

Mind if I turn this into a brand?

Because that is everyone's *That's the New Me*

in the scrolls of the click economy.

Velvet under-gland,

earning your burgeoning person-*ishness*, please

reverse-clap if you can hear me.

Yeah, no.   Send a grief bio.

Zygote, Life Speck,

  Love's Lunk: forgive.

I was late out all night

    jumpstarting verbs

       against new-world numbness.

  We're each of us going

to have to arrive somewhere: *Come as you are,*

  cute as an *it*.

    Each day

    I personate

    mystery copies

    of yesterday's me.

Midnight's pip,

  have I mentioned I'm calving

    one whale

  of a molten pre-afterlife,

munching Puget Sound salmon douched out *au jus* with Chinook cocaine?

You ever sung "Kumbaya" in Creole?

  Do you think it's nice to futz

    with spec consciousness?

      Is a shish kabob fissionable?

Dear Celly.

I urge
my niece
to nurse at least

the seven proton-*riche* excitements per
average monthly eighth square inch.

Make it through one day,

you can make it to death.

Some dragoness app

is trying to get me to tape this.

Dear Z,

The collective brain's

migrated

to spectacle pit,

the world in its

permanent warfare suits,   its plague of blue angers,

reality's X-outs

inking edits in time

with electronic shocks   and superlatives   teamed

with bland resplendent bursts
of personhood-arson. *Ou* redeem this
blow-kiss as one type of TSA PreCheck swipe
on your not-yet-a-barcode.
XXX. *Muah!* and namaste
anyhow, *Not-it-nigh-kid,* 'cause
we merge in verse.

Now then. Are you of a mind

to try on

this tight little fishskin?

Pray-telling is poetry's birthplace. Do.

Would you rather real-life swim

or live-stream?

Last question: perfection

of the life or of the work?

Answer me   in heaped first-person Earth.

III

Dear Zeitgeist

Dear Z,

New Zealand views animals by law
not as objects but sentient beings.

And now this river, Te Awa Tupua,
revered by the Maori,

is in parliament's eyes
endowed with hominid dignity.

Here on out, this great river
dips its finned hides into the human—

that vehemence field,
that ruckus of feeling-tone—

mountain to sea, including bit tributaries.
This gently evolved,

heaving torsion now may refer
his and her agents

to court: two lawyers,
one from the *Iwi* tribe; the other,

the government.
Mere Zygote—

my vein-wired squirt
of sperm-and-egg union:

seed || ovum
XX || XY

Cells || *Self* —
your status already

a conflict zone
to the tune

of a great ape's girth.
Reverie's boygirl,

hey, do you think
right now is the time

to suggest
you go find yourself—

there in your unlit foyer—
two bang-up members of the bar?

Dear Z,

Today I will call you *Conceptus*
because it evokes a more inclusive world,

the kind that invites placenta
and fetus, amnion, yolk sac:

the full-on palpation,
fertilization to birth—that zero-point field

where what is finite
latches onto the divine.

This page, to take a single instance,
was a ticking blank

till all at once the whole house
starts to catenate its parts

toward implantation
and then language breaks me

into acting as its host—
the same way you sneaked in

to moor a smidgen-dome
inside my niece. Believe.

Flesh is the not-me
I peacock around in:

part of a schtick
to try and keep

the people *persons*.
Dear Zeitgeist.

Whatever
one dips in the sea

instantly crusts up
with life.

Yankee Conceptus,

serene mesh
of speculative kin,

have I mentioned
that I keep a stream

of ongoing lines
to you on my cell?

      I   *Yes*   *You*

are always the first three words
below the blank notepad

the phone's grey rectangles
daily suggest-rush to me.

Dear Rich Jam,

Today, Crayola said goodbye to *Dandelion;*
sugar is more dangerous than gunpowder,

and meditation at home on the mutating world
is the new sex. I sit in my room until I'm laid flat

by language's hum tones. The world glooms
as I try to live out the slowest year of my prime,

despite the cell phone's horse-nosing in
to headline this notice: *Serena Williams*

Is Pregnant and *Keep Your Own Egg Cells*
Fresh with Epigenetics. Alphabet is a firm

on the Nasdaq, and according to this receipt,
I just saved $98.46 by borrowing books

from the Kooskia Library. *Ou* sometimes the sounds
of a word will openly text me its curves. Forgive:

I feel on a bit of a dopamine high.
We each swap molecules for new ones

all the time, which means to understand someone
you have to become them. Our shared inner ear

aches for low sounds that have no counterpart
in words, and yes, as tested by *Ancestry.com,*

Zygote, like you, I'm basically a little everyone.
For each of whom I've come to feel

vaguely *parental.* It's *prenatal's* anagram.
As *verse* is *serve's.* The *b* is a *p* singing baritone.

Dear Z,

Someday I'll be able to type to you
with only my brain;

people will hear through their skin
like a dog who might whine

through its brow or see with its withers.
Zygote, by then, you'll have ensconced

yourself in the hulls of canoes
called *Becoming Human* —

machines tuned
to flesh out

your mute simulacrum,
grow noses to groom you.

Or maybe you will have fled
this herd sphere, having intuited truths

about incorporation:
It tries to steal my you *from me,*

you may well have sung
had you swiped in

to go on.

It's a bit of a koan.

Dear Z,

It's August-hot for June—the locust leaves
cinched tight in shiftless air,

the anxious state of the U.S.
pre-stressing babies in the womb.

Science says: *Any is many,*
and when we cue ourselves

to other people's blues,
we do it with the brain's

right hemisphere. Life Speck,
here is where you'd tell me I'd do well

to lay hands on a linked attention helmet—
if you knew to talk—since now I want to bring up

zombie metaphors to peg impending civil death.
Well, *Zompire* is the portmanteau

for left brain's zest for power. That, plus
it portends exactly how the merging lordigarchs

intend to zonk and drain
all beauty from our baited crania.

Not something someone's plum
pre-human wants to read about

in popup books or pages
    you can stick your index through

        to make a barn horse finger-dance.
Still, I figured you should know.

So many things seem locked
in an emergent state,

and language only ever lays uncertain eggs
inside my craw.

These lurid days
it does so with such stately calm

I take the time to claim it for my own.

Dear Z,

When earliest humans adopted the skin
      and stones of language, they received

a parallel DNA. Limited syllable-tones
      are nucleic acids. Yoke and cleave: They serve

as linkage-salve that helps us stay in touch.
      Instead of DNA's four-base structure,

English serves up 44. It's how many sounds
      our syllables can ape. And talking with others

just revs the genes' velour headsets
      that make us want to speak to ourselves.

How this evolves is probably somewhere
      a novel in progress—all *mama* and mouth-

spore. Need, plus its mimetic software.
      In the mother lives the other: *O her.*

Zygote, I have been sent here to tell you
      the deal in modernity's thus:

the orderly outsource of *chi* to handheld devices,
      the offshore of memory to the machine,

a market/self coupling—the rich in
      their rogue protections from empathy.

Dear Pulse. To love is to stump for a shit-ton
      of worry. And not for nothing, dear bitsy

aquanaut, does the cell phone's notes app
      now start with   *Are   you   we*

Dear Life Speck,

As we speak, or as I type to you
and you divide-concede,

disrupter and disinformation bots
work overtime. *Autofill* | | *Autocrat :*
Ctrl+Z, yes, the country

swerves its Humvee
across living hope—
the whole place

having moored its fiction-dome
in ire's simplicity.
In language gated

by circles of
certainty.
My thinking is

that you should still
relax and take this
to be the pregnancy test

of some more curative order—
Regale | | *Unveil* : Dear Z,
I feel your frank need

to womb
into some zone
like a song in a movie. Believe.

When we spend time rightly
in sync,
we become mind's

twin smithereens, and
I feel I am maybe
finally a jinn

or have founded a gender
unbeknownst to anyone
before—a Doe Ridge Trail

who skeins a way
through the world
in the frame of a girl

who joneses
for hominoid rivers
and mule deer.

Who jouks to the ongoing
chink of rain's bones
set to the strings of the clan tongue.

Listen.

Lately, events hack into
the shank of my nights
while mornings,

meadowlarks choir—all
for the sake of these missives to you.
Whether I pipe of that day-moon

as cloud or coin
whose clarity terrifies,
or moon of how daily warzones

might well re-hum you,
let me just say
this eon's gizmos

frack the peak mammalian
ministry of *presence*.
Still, Zygote,

lucky for *Oh   You   Yes*

there's such a thing
as pre-chills
caused by the slowest

movement of words
through the sacs and roots
and sheaths

of those not-yet
arm hairs—under
the duress of missing limbs.

Dear Z,

I am here to wave you *hulloo*
on the plank of a day that asks me

to freeze all attempts to *other* Aunt Autofill—
that alt-ozone, that madre word beer,

that weirdo mad-lib who likes to clank bread
with the inner *doyenne*

who serves as our *You   I   Us,*
an experienced innocence—yes,

maybe no more than a pilfered blues riff
from some zona pellucida.

> *Phone   write   home*
> *Teeth   true   lines,*

the wee machine blips. Among other things,
I've contracted a baby who sells me this too:

how such finical music is mostly a product
of time and dentition: *helper   world   best,*

the machine cellos in. Am shitting you not.
Such symbiosis *perfect   point   dates*

what sums up Beethoven. ... So
I loathe the noun "teamwork"—

> *see   us   we*
> *people speak game*

but it's what inserted words here at hand

      say are so *worth the freak*
      we must *train effort thus.*

You could say I contradict myselves.
Ironic | | *Oneiric* : Still, how suggest

elsewise of *Am er I ~~ Her yes am,*
that nattery cell line queering our handhold

on everything coiled or neural or
pixeled — ready, on cue, to be world?

Zygote,

Between the world and me
is mind's lining.

Between the word
and you,

uterine wall. Beyond that,
persons slip

between states—so many
cells' émigrés.

Dear Z,

in the presence
of your latency—

that vacant shoe,
those shades

of facelessness—
let's say

I think I feel
the sound of dots moving.

IV

The X Y and Zs

Dear Zero,

Modern humans evolved only once—in what's likely
East Africa, 200,000 years ago. So don't freak

when I shout out *We share the same mama*:
Mitochondrial Eve. Unlike the one in the Garden

of Eden, mtEve was not the sole woman on Earth,
but the one who made her descent into everyone.

So pray tell, teensy homunculus, as the line
from "Time of the Season" by The Zombies,

that British Invasion band, goes: *Who's your daddy?*

Please know that should you come be, Big Data
will quickly conceive you as processing stream,

a more or less numeral entity—lacking internal lyric:
that giddiest hymnal. That solemn bee. The think-feeling

fist that is *inwit*. Queerest iota, does this kind of talk
smack of hokum-humanist seething on my part?

Our shared mother mtEve was mostly a kink of statistics,
a ringing quark of a person: a true lovely, who probably

knew to venerate horses. How to grow manifold leaves.
Not sure how this will relate, but in Sanskrit *datta* means

give, and The Zombies go on to wonder if your daddy's rich
or if he's taken any time // to show you what you need

to live. They want to know your name. *Tell it to me slowly.*
It's time to show—with pleasured hands—how love runs.

Dear Zygote + Dear Mother mtEve,
The visiting baby is one spiny mimic machine.

When I curl my tongue to a tube, she does so too.
Which circles back to The Zombies, who borrowed

from Big Mama Thornton and copied Sam Cooke,
who had the good sense to mother-queeg young

Dionne Warwick when they were on gospel circuit.
Dear mtEve. *Y*-chromosome genes will decay over time,

then get lost from the genome. Ah, the felled world
is a chain gang of partnership blues and peculiarity—

corner ad selling its physics of tans while the garbled
mathematics of racism sizzles—*continually* | | *continuously;*

that | |*which; bring* | | *take; copy* | | *take over.* The Fake
Zombies were what is called a Con Rock Band:

four Texas boys imitating that British group
touring America. ... **Psych!**

I was told they were only a studio sound,
one of them said: *A series of booths and tracks,*

maybe a Hammond organ or two.
They wore huge cowboy hats in their press shots.

We just made what we were making,
they would insist, flying V guitars strung up in bars

like Whisky A Go-Go,
faring no worse than the fake Archies—who jacked

the cartoon—or the pre-punk band Question Mark
and the Mysterians. Whose members, it's high time

　　　I add, Dear Zy and Queen Mother mtEve,
were children of migrant farmers en route

　　　to Michigan just to pick crops—the original
name of this band having been *? and the X Y and Zs.*

Zygote,

No machine will ever be capable of doing x.
What the x stands for depends on the level

pelvis who makes the request. Combining
simple states of *and, or,* and *not* creates

complex chains of logical reasoning,
whose task is to ace the next newness.

Ask Amy. Ask the best line judge. Ask
Joseph Campbell, who likened all AI

to Old Testament Gods: Lots of rules
and || *not* one shot of mercy. *Lotsa Lots' Lotteries* :

It's *now's* new democracy. Or:
If you *datta*-give notepad "Lots," it sends you

Loads of Lord Loyalty. ... To be human today
simply means data can trim you to theorem,

regimes that egg on equality's
interstate ecstasies—out; immortality, in—

for the few, thanks to tweaked
biochemistry. *Rational* || *Imaginary*

And-or-not's fingerling: So, routine submersible
You Yes Maybe — Life Speck, you're going

to have to admit: That wack number e is one
you really could show off some *give* to.

Dear Z,

People also ask

What is one i?

Can an imaginary number be rational?

Can something real also be infinite?

What is the i equal to in math?

Zy, it's high time I mention I'm sweet on the face
in your voice, even though you have neither.

And | | *or* : Just to be clear, I do most of our talking.
The ear mewls and throws shards that know how

to ape the whole human drapery. Which makes
the full lexical system kind of like IBM's Watson,

whose joy was to beat two bipedals at Jeopardy.
What is Elegance? was a base query it knew to be

The Correct Answer. Then it buzzed the right question to:
Those who stand up might still be asleep from this.

"What *isn't* sleep-walking," I'd like to ask Alex Trebek,
"in the ongoing state of the outer world's id?" —

if such a place can be said to exist. Even so, Zy-
Speck, the wages of language is eggs-old rebirth

for any Jane Doe who thinks maybe to clothe
her next day within arches of trees, or scramble

all dirt to raku. BTW, *Anthimeria*'s the anthem-word
for sprucing the world into new grammatical shape:

the way nouns flip to action words, how *heart* beats
as verb: It's how adjectives arc into paper planes.

It's how I'll gazelle from the solid to vapor state.
How a zygote *plein-airs* its hot load of humanity ammo.

Hi Zy—

You could say I've been slothing, low-key
   doing laundry as I spill vowels toward the face

of the visiting baby. *Utopia, Euphonia, Eunomia.*
   Oiseau, French for *bird,* buys all the vowels.

As does *Aotearoa*—almost: the Maori word for *Island*
   of the Long White Cloud we also know as New Zealand.

The sounds in *Aotearoa* are so *religious temple,*
   our lobes row driven oars toward where

that tiny *ear* lies centrally entombed.
   Dear missive. Language is destiny-mistress,

so keep your curving tympanum pre-tuned:
   Whoever abuses the word bruises the air,

bullies the grain of the earth, then moves up to captain
   of Stateship: some maniac shogun. Meanwhile,

my fab humaneer, this primate-typhoon
   strapped in a green high chair keeps turning her head

so far round her tawny-owl neck that I think I hear
   space-time snap in her artery linings. Oh,

Oiseau-ape, euphony's boy toy, I'm trying to lay out
   a something I'll call here a start-up republic,

which mother-idea incubated through
   mostly the blear of my thumbs. Between you

and me, *ou* Baby, I just have to ask: What
   might be the animal-word for *No not some nutso*

warrior system, for *One infant teething drips*
    hologram maps on a bib, for *Science needs cell lines,*

for *blues,* for *Anthimeria,* for *dread,* for *Sudoku,*
    for *No—not more oil?* To signal these, sputter a clean spit

of horse snort. Unbend an old sea shanty.
    Strawberry forth some keener strip of word.

Zy,

When I try to reenter the world, it wicks me away.
Get back to your room: Language insists

that I live at its hipbone. Late nights, to fight back,
I dig words from their graves like *wanhope*

and *inwit*. This teaches some things to Aunt/
Uncle Autofill—tetchy old crone + Mr. Guess Man,

that somewhat hot mess of a sycophant-
orphan who knows his/her own lack of home

in the late Fertile Crescent. *Mesopotamia.*
Life Speck, if/when you can, say it. And often.

————————

You'll feel its cuneiform's sexual vestures,
which here and there trip up a sadness shot in

by the gods' roaring hip guns. Hear ye! I recently
dated this cowboy/war veteran, whose lone brand

of Ranger-despair meant he knew how to shiv
the doe moon with a chip of martini glass.

His thumbs snagged the V-lines in six of my dresses.
Which amounted to scenes of *geomor* beauty.

This is Old English for just how he sat there alone,
sad of mind, as he shot tender looks into me.

————————

How does anyone know how to say anything? I asked
of the blank summer beer the last time

he twizzled my hair in the nesting petunias.
How so uneven a world makes avuncular bots

take the humming word *earth* for its animus *war*
tends to weary one's hopes. BTW,

Cwide is the Oldenday senile noun for *decree*.
For *speech. Saying. Judgment. Will. Testament*:

a strongly masculine term, sweet Homie,
I haven't a clue how to begin to pronounce.

Dear Z,

Your Georgia aunt could not pronounce *idea*

in such a way it did not end in *ear*.

Dear Z,

Today I woke with a great ape in my heart who told me, *On the sheet of paper Mind lies flat: The grace of statecraft starts by lying low.* Don't ask me how my ape knows that. It's a dime-thin line between me and the next world, soul and bonobo. Dear Life-Frack. It's just me here laying out the alphabet by ear, all the while hangin' with this Old World hominoidea. You feel me? Oh, and if you don't mind my suddenly mixing species, on the subject of greatness of polity I'll try to quote Vergil: *Ulla apis, nulla apis,* or *One bee is no bee.* Yes, the one true dream is to become Nobody—this quakey note, some body-politic machine that you and me—yeah, no—should lie apart together sticking quarters in until the internet swells to the girth of the sun, and Sun, she grows so fat and grody-old, she finally blows.

Zygote, you should enjoy your limniad state,
nymph-like and windless, there on two sides

of a threshold. Howsoever, the WordHippo
wonders if I mean to speak *lemonade.*

This saké is murky, and it makes me wish
I could tottle off to that original somewhere

in whom even the wines sip words
and live alphabets draw on that spliff

of night air. … Life Speck, here
is the ordinal pregnancy:

Without each other, we hole up
within each other. Remember, too,

I have been busy, turning
the soil in the few people's hearts

I plan to rename the grave
when my day comes: am hoping to sow

the silt-line conditions for a happy death—
choired by Husband *Consciousness*—

that wry spirit-vegetable. That solid air
loyalty. Netflix, elsewhere,

boots into verb, while power lopes in
to daily un-heaven everyone. Still,

for the most part, Ms. Zygote Missive,
you are the test of the great human *maybe,*

there in that mother-hip meadow —
that namelessly face-free state

of *between*. Dear nymph-dividual:
Let me not spew lemonade,

as I've gotten wind of your balls-out greed
for the good of all species.

V

Forgive, Relieve

Dear Life Speck,

The world lets you take things in through holes
in the face, which means I can say something

like *Vagus is a nerve that calms my words,*
The I *is a swinging door,*

and *Just to pass the afternoon,*
my eyes massaged these seven breathy horses

as I sat still on this lazy knoll.
Here and there I must take time

to bow down to the river birch
and stroke its nosy care, salute its hair-end

plots to re-sync *nation*—catkins waving
thank you notes to those majorities

who knew to just hang on.
Ou the age is strange as a lei

of screaming butterflies.
The public hip has heart dysplasia,

and the *now* is this frank necropolis
of razor wire and gated garden beds.

To counter this means
everyone must come to see

all residents as members of *my group*—
the pain of others,

our severest strand of anguish:
fiber || string   coil || tendril :

Oracular Z,
sometimes you just want to walk

toward the arms
of the moans from that oncoming tuba.

Dear Z,

To ancestor over the visiting baby is to lay foot
in a land of perpetual symbol. Is to exist

on both sides of the living ravine, the way that to sit
and sing-write is to lean into the death of time—

the rational imaginary *End* || *And* :
Doing so lays me flat in the earliest place

here on Earth and the most *fertile*—after which word
AutoFill Tarzan-types *Earth   Land   Woman,*

as if in caveperson bass. Zygote, there is this thing
called the Aquatic Ape Hypothesis, which rests

on the thought that what makes us human—speech,
lack of thick fur, and walking upright—evolved

through a 10-million-year period, when Africa
got flat-out soaked, and our forbears were coaxed to

live waterside. A notion foregrounding breath control,
soft body parts, loss of vibrissae, plus finally

the needs and roles of females and babies—
as counter to theories of warrior-hunters.

In 1960, national papers broadcast this headline:
"Oxford Prof Says Man a Sea Ape," for which

he caught boatloads of flak from his coworkers. Zy,
the world's pretty colicky. You've no doubt deduced

it hides balled handfuls of dirt in its fat folds.
Life Speck, if this helps bring you to term, *ta-da!*:

Every tale is the working out of a premise in tones
we call words—*premise* long ago having oozed

from the feminine Latin for *send before*.
Miss Pilgrim Missive—O wholly provisional baby,

before I mail this to you, here's the real scoop:
All day I incubate sounds to be newly carnated.

Dear Life Speck,

When I sing "Blackbird" to the visiting baby,
her fingers hook sounds from my mouth

and fist them into furies of clay.
What have I in common

with most living things, and how
do I differ? is the main question

that blinkers her boundary conditions.
She dung-beetles along,

the human experiment grafting its skin
onto madcap austerity, corporations

the nation's trophy constituents, prisons
harvesting children for profit—

the whole system sounding
its moves toward the sea-lurch

of language's overturn. Men sublimate
anguish through punishment modes—

the doomed blackbird practically tearing
its beak as it sinks its rolled hymns in blank

heartbreak of night. Hear this. Who will not
feel his own pain can only inflict it.

Visiting pilgrim, to plainly despair
is to sip on the milk of the great human braille:

its tender uprisings. Its horripilation—
that's gooseflesh—

if it so happens you were awaiting
some new takeaway on that '68 standard.

Dear Z,

I'm tempted to *cc* you when I think
of how my fists feel six months pregnant

almost all the time,
or of the ways some microorganisms

in our blood must lie in wait
for one blind chance

to chew each other up. Why, just today
I couldn't stop from telling Jane,

my favorite neighbor, off.
I ignored the warning *Every Word Counts*

issued by a woman's orange T-shirt
at the Y. ... The scream with Jane

buzz-cut my best genetic code.
Forgive | | *Relieve* :

If time were alphabet's
grapevine, I'd place myself at *V*,

the village vessel. Veterinarian
to a lone sea squirt.

The rangy *vaquero* of love's ovum,
the untried vizard of a recomposed *we*.

Still, Zygote, you could write a book
on my misdeeds, nestled

in your gene-zipped envelope.

My Dear Migrating Cells.
Dear Sigh to Whom I Send. Dear Sorry Note.

Dear Fetal DNA: My Blind CC.
My Dear *Mesdames, Messieurs*.

Hello Dear Team.
My Dear Mz Z.

Dear *Voix Humaine*:
Oh please. Just sit here with me.

Dear Z,

Sometimes I think I should sink my thoughts
      straight into you instead of writing them down,

the way my appaloosa, Melville,
      slips his never-notes to me: *I have survived*

for millions of years by hiding all weakness,
      suggests his jugular groove as he jerks

his hock joint, and his holy brown feathers
      of fetlock hair lend the blanched foothill

its full-blown leg up on joy. You feel me?
      Dear Preface to Breath: Please

let me list off a horse's prime features
      as my means to reach you—clairvoyance

to shore up your bonding-urge circuitry:
      pastern, hock; hoof, rump dock; barrel,

withers. Elbow. Ergot. Dear Omen.
      Dear Whoa Boy, hey,

luck-of-the-nosebag's soft ESP:
      Psst! Dear Butter Nugget.

"Alexithymia" claims it's the word for
      having no feel for the inner experience, one's own

or another's. You maybe could call it the *now's*
      diagnosis. The autumn oil's opposite. To try

and put a halt to it is my spotted horse's daily
      white whale. *Roving | | Raving. …*

Forgive me for mixing giant animals mid-trope.
        Forget my rangy trespasses,

forgive sensation's ill-timed ovulations
        this October afternoon—its orange-*ish* yellows,

its plump rosehips—as I leave
        to canter Melville toward the Dry Creek Ridge.

Dear Z,

Giving a gift is the basis for language,
the heart's hip beat: *Arrive* || *Survive* :

Zygote, I need not tell you. There's nothing
like the act of steering molten thought

through scrawled throat-tones as a means
to graft a whole new earth to things—

even with the eon's known supposing
over ends to all our days. Listen.

Planet X News had scheduled the *Zed*
of this world for just about now.

American Zee, still,
there you are,

lope-stroke of Zorro. That
sibilant mid-*Mozart*.

Divisible mote
on time's moonlit tambourine.

Therefore, I need not tell you
the letter Z has not always meant *tail*

of the alphabet—that moody wind instrument.
That allograph beauty, whose fevering ether

croons atop naked frailty's tines.
Turns out the ampersand,

that *in itself and,*
is what used to spell

the ABC's end: & thus
you should home in on how it is, yes,

such a pisser that profit is gift from the poor
to the rich. And so in the zombie apocalypse

the Zumwalt-class destroyer is what comes
to mind as my weapon of choice—

which ship I would use to take down caste.
O Z, it's a swank can of worms to seize

a beat at all. This sole fact makes my heart
bird toward the towhead mountains.

Excite || *Unite : and per se and* et & so.
So. What might be zygote argot for *Just sayin'*?

Dear Z,

I stayed awake all night to make sure
     I didn't die in my sleep. It's a thing

among folks at point *V* on the vine.
     Besides, it's when I binge-think best—

when the gut finds a home in its deep
     feather-guessing. Midnight Z,

if something G-rated-sexy
     is needed to keep your attention,

I'll admit the word *zoism*
     is one I could crush on for days,

since it knows to show beasts can boast
     mutable power. And maybe the couplet

will prove the sultriest spined team around—
     time's consummate pair skaters—

in the meanwhile, *person* comes uncoupled
     from the rank of *citizen*. And just because

I stayed awake, some living verb
     dared me to stage my most fierce

inner fights in the nude. So I did:
     Z, is you is

          or is you ain't
               Ameri-pire's endpoint?

. . .

That's all hella schizzy, Screenage Zy
might sometime come to say,

not to mention that right now we're both
probably stowed inside some volatile TV.

Ou I fear

I am way misaligned
with most sets

of the norm-cloning world.

Because I fear, I blow cold

when I notice

the breath falling out

into fraidy-toe reason.

I sweat beer

at how just being moneyed

might soon mark the order of person

slated to last,
then I mainline despair.

And per say and

End-And

Listen, Superorganism.

Dear Mammalian I:

I find when I enter the fear,
I totally freak out the rhythms.

Life Speck,

The alphabet's perfectly fitted
to gum-reef and tooth. Any baby knows

only an imbecile fails to eat books.
Translation: We are the noises

we pore over, glyphs we *salaam*
and lip-read, which surge from that EpiPen

no one person owns. This gets me
to thinking—a sidebar note—

of every square, screened thing's
numbing of time. Of whether the mind

might rather live in a place called *Eunomia.*
It's Greek for *Goddess of Order's Good Laws*

and Green Pastures. What's more,
it's a large stony asteroid,

the strength of whose orbit
stays with me—clear as the face

of the person-gorilla that novelist knew
to dub *Ishmael.* Call me

a helping-vowel's noob drama queen,
but *Eunomia's* silent *e* swings

as this dashing irrational number
whose rife liminality

ships me to Queequeg.
Which serves to tap

something I crave. Dear Listen.
I'll give you how some scenes in life

might still fall in line—

but at the brink level
of emblem or myth.

And how even an unpeopled Idaho
may end up this wow-state to live

if you're big into seas of dry land
and open-vowel euphony policies,

where the poet is known to be
cowboy of wild rye and the open page,

riding out trails on a word called *horse*,
raveling its earths in some human disguise.

Postscript

Whereas *being* is *begin*'s anagram *&* again is *binge*'s.
Wherein a being beginning living notes the *not to*.
Wherefore to begin living at all or to *come to*.
Whereupon the lip of truth,

Dear &:

Not to begin living is never even.

Notes:

pp. 18 and 60: "Queeg" is a neologism: a verb that means to hug or to grab something (or someone) strongly but warmly—in *Queequeg*-like fashion, as per this passage from the first paragraph of chapter four of *Moby-Dick*: "Indeed, partly lying on it as the arm did when I first awoke, I could hardly tell it from the quilt, they so blended their hues together; and it was only by the sense of weight and pressure that I could tell that Queequeg was hugging me."

p. 90: This *Ishmael* reference points to Daniel Quinn's 1992 work of philosophical fiction.

About the Author

Diane Raptosh's fourth book of poetry, *American Amnesiac* (Etruscan Press), was longlisted for the 2013 National Book Award and was a finalist for the Housatonic Book Award. The recipient of three fellowships in literature from the Idaho Commission on the Arts, she served as the Boise Poet Laureate (2013) as well as the Idaho Writer-in-Residence (2013-2016), the highest literary honor in the state. In 2018 she received the Idaho Governor's Arts Award in Excellence. A highly active ambassador for poetry, she has given poetry workshops everywhere from riverbanks to maximum security prisons. She teaches creative writing and runs the program in Criminal Justice/Prison Studies at The College of Idaho. Her most recent collection of poems, *Human Directional*, was released by Etruscan Press in 2016.

Books from Etruscan Press

Etruscan Press Is Proud of Support Received From

Wilkes University

Youngstown State University

The Ohio Arts Council

The Stephen & Jeryl Oristaglio Foundation

The Nathalie & James Andrews Foundation

The National Endowment for the Arts

The New Mexico Community Foundation

Founded in 2001 with a generous grant from the Oristaglio Foundation, Etruscan Press is a nonprofit cooperative of poets and writers working to produce and promote books that nurture the dialogue among genres, achieve a distinctive voice, and reshape the literary and cultural histories of which we are a part.

etruscan press
www.etruscanpress.org
Etruscan Press books may be ordered from

Consortium Book Sales and Distribution
800.283.3572
www.cbsd.com

Etruscan Press is a 501(c)(3) nonprofit organization.
Contributions to Etruscan Press are tax deductible
as allowed under applicable law.
For more information, a prospectus,
or to order one of our titles,
contact us at books@etruscanpress.org.